Maths Matters!

Size

Look out for these sections to help you learn more about each topic:

Remember…
This provides a summary of the key concept(s) on each two-page entry. Use it to revise what you have learnt.

Word check
These are new and important words that help you understand the ideas presented on each two-page entry.

All of the word check entries in this book are shown in the glossary on pages 44 to 48. The versions in the glossary are sometimes more extensive explanations.

Book link…
Although this book can be used on its own, other titles in the *Maths Matters!* set may provide more information on certain topics. This section tells you which other titles to refer to.

Place value

To make it easy for you to see exactly what we are doing, you will find coloured columns behind the numbers in all the examples on this and the following pages. This is what the colours mean:

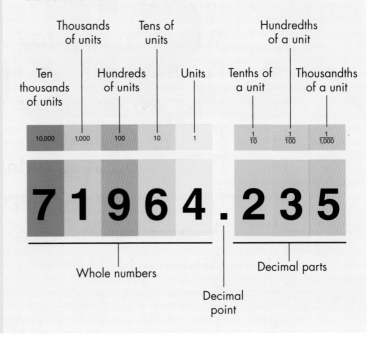

An Atlantic Europe Publishing Book

Series concept by *Brian Knapp and Duncan McCrae*
Text contributed by *Brian Knapp and Colin Bass*
Design and production by *Duncan McCrae*
Illustrations of characters by *Nicolas Debon*
Digital illustrations by *David Woodroffe*
Other illustrations by *Peter Bull Art Studio*
Editing by *Lorna Gilbert and Barbara Carragher*
Layout by *Duncan McCrae and Mark Palmer*
Reprographics by *Global Colour*
Printed and bound by *LEGO SpA, Italy*

Copyright © 1999
Atlantic Europe Publishing Company Limited

First published in 1999 by
Atlantic Europe Publishing Company Limited,
Greys Court Farm, Greys Court,
Henley-on-Thames, Oxon, RG9 4PG, UK.

Suggested cataloguing location
Size – *Maths Matters!* set, volume 9
  Geometrical constructions – Juvenile literature
  Knapp, Brian and Bass, Colin
  516.1'5

ISBN 1 862140 41 3

Picture credits
All photographs are from the *Earthscape Editions* photolibrary.

This book is manufactured from sustainable managed forests. For every tree cut down at least one more is planted.

The 13 volumes in the *Maths Matters!* set are:

Contents

Introduction

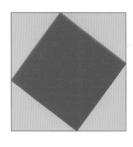

$$a = \pi r^2$$

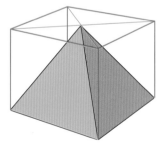

Many things around us come in a wide variety of sizes. In this book you will learn how to measure and work with the sizes of things.

The sizes we use most often are length, area, volume and angle. For example, we often need to work out the length of a boundary of a flat shape. We also often want to know the size of an area inside the boundary.

People who are designing and building things need to know how to measure angles accurately.

$$a = \ell \times w$$

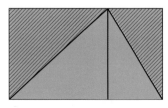

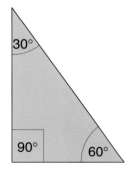

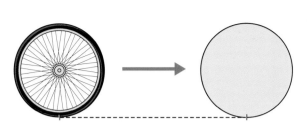

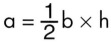

$$a = \frac{1}{2}b \times h$$

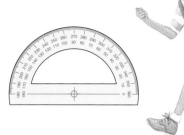

$$\pi = \frac{22}{7}$$

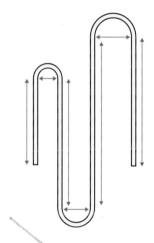

When we have solid objects like blocks or hollow objects like bottles, we often want to know their volume, or how much they hold – their capacity.

Finding out about sizes has only a few simple rules, and some smart tricks that save time and allow us to check our answers.

You will find that, by following the stage by stage approach of this book, it will be easy to learn how to find out about sizes. As each idea is set out on a separate page, you can always refer back to an idea if you temporarily forget it.

$$90° + 30° + 60° = 180°$$

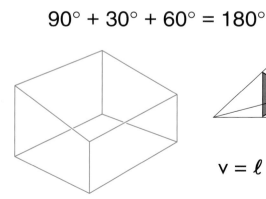

$$v = \ell \times w \times h$$

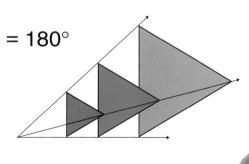

What is a perimeter?

Think of any shape you like – a piece of paper, a field, the surface of a lake or a country – each of these things has a line marking its edge. This is the boundary of the shape. Mathematicians call the length of a boundary the perimeter. Here are some examples of boundaries and perimeters.

This historic farm uses a fence to mark out its boundary. The perimeter is the length of the fence. The farmer might want to find the length of the perimeter if he were thinking of renewing the fence, because he would need to know how many lengths of timber to order from the timber yard.

This is a running track. The perimeter is made of straight and curved sections. The total perimeter of many international running tracks is **400** metres.

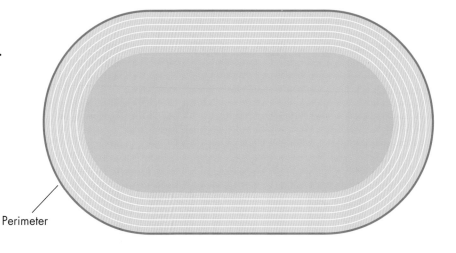

Perimeter

This is the boundary of a block. Joggers who live in the block might want to know the perimeter of the block so that they could work out how many times they have to jog around the block to complete a 1-kilometre or a 1-mile circuit.

Perimeter

This is a map of Norway. The length of the perimeter is over **5,000** km (**3,000** miles). It is so long because the perimeter includes all the ins and outs of the coast.

Remember... The boundary is the edge. It may be straight, curved or a mixture of both. The perimeter is the total distance all the way around a flat shape.

Word check

Boundary: The line or curve separating the inside of the shape you are interested in from everything outside it.

Perimeter: The size of the boundary of a flat object. It is the distance once around it.

Perimeters can take on many shapes

The perimeter is simply the length of a boundary. This tells us nothing about its shape. In fact you can find many different shapes with the same perimeter. Here are a few of them. The perimeter in each case is **100** units.

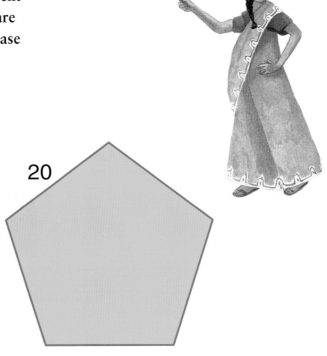

The shape to the right has five straight sides of equal length. It is called a pentagon. Each straight length is the same, and is:

$$\frac{100}{5} = 20 \text{ units long}$$

This shape to the right is called a rectangle. It has two pairs of straight sides. It is **40** units long and **10** units wide. The perimeter is:

$$40 + 40 + 10 + 10 = 100$$

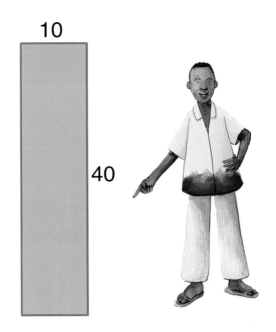

The shape below is long and thin. It contains very little space inside it. The perimeter is:

$$1 + 7 + 7 + 14 + 14 + 10 + 8 + 17 + 6 + 6 + 5 + 4 + 1 = 100$$

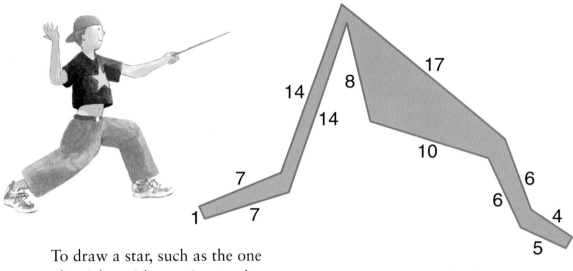

To draw a star, such as the one on the right, with a perimeter that is exactly **100** units, how long must each line in the star be?

To find this out we need to notice that the star has **20** 'rays'.

If the perimeter of the star is to be **100** units, then each ray must be ½₀ of the perimeter of **100** units.

$$1 \text{ ray} = \frac{100}{20} = 5$$

But each ray is made up of two lines. So each line of the star is:

$$\frac{5}{2} = 2.5 \text{ units long}$$

These two lines make a ray.

Remember... Many different shapes can have the same perimeter.

Book link... Find out more about fractions and decimals in the books *Fractions* and *Decimals* in the *Maths Matters!* set.

Word check
Pair: Two things which match up in some way.

Perimeters of squares and rectangles

Squares and rectangles are straight-sided shapes with four right angles.

In both cases the opposite sides are parallel and have the same length. As a result we can find the perimeter of a rectangle simply by measuring two touching sides and doubling the total.

In the case of a square, because the sides are all the same length, it is even simpler to find the perimeter, as you will see below.

Square

The perimeter of a square is the sum of the lengths of all four sides.
For the square on the right this is:

$$3 + 3 + 3 + 3 = 12$$

However, all four sides are the same length. Remembering that multiplication is a quick way of adding the same number many times, we can write:

$$4 \times 3 = 12$$

Now we can write a formula which allows us to find the perimeter of a square if we know just one length. Suppose the length of the side we know is represented by the letter s, and the perimeter by the letter p. Then the formula is:

The red line is the boundary, or **perimeter** (p), of this yellow square.

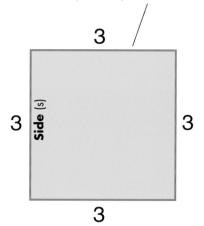

Four times one side equals the perimeter

$$4 \times s = p$$

This could also be written:

$$p = 4 \times s$$

Check that the formula works by putting 3 for s and 12 for p.

Rectangle

The perimeter of a rectangle is the sum of the length of all four sides. In a rectangle the two pairs of sides are of different lengths. In this diagram you can see that one pair of sides is **3** units long, whereas the other pair is **7** units long. The perimeter is

$$3 + 7 + 3 + 7 = 20$$

We have two 3's and two 7's, so we can write the perimeter as:

$$2 \times 3 + 2 \times 7 = 20$$

Notice that if you were travelling around the rectangle, you would be halfway around when you had completed one short side and one long side.

Suppose the length of the short side is represented by the letter **w** (for width) and the length of the long side by the letter ℓ (for length). If we call the perimeter **p**, as before, then the formula is:

$$p = 2 \, (w + \ell)$$

This is another way of writing

$$p = (2 \times w) + (2 \times \ell)$$

Check that the formula works by putting 7 for ℓ, 3 for w and 20 for p.

Remember... A single letter can be used in a formula to stand for a measurement. The formula can then be used again and again with different numbers replacing the letter.

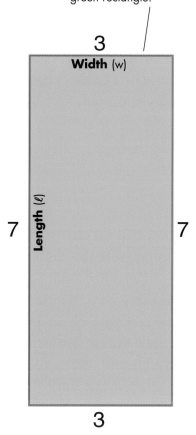

The red line is the boundary, or **perimeter** (p), of this green rectangle.

3

Width (w)

7   Length (ℓ)   7

3

Word check:

Equation: A number sentence using the = symbol, telling us that two different ways of writing a number are the same. For example, $2 + 2 = 4$ and $9 - 5 = 4$.

Formula: A rule for calculating something. It is often an equation containing a letter or several letters.

Parallel: Parallel lines are lines which will remain the same distance apart for ever.

Rectangle: A four-sided shape in which pairs of opposite sides are the same length and all four corners are right angles.

Right angle: An angle which is exactly a quarter of a complete turn.

Square: A regular rectangle with all four sides the same length and four angles of equal size.

Perimeter of a circle

The perimeter of a circle is called the circumference.

You cannot use a straight edge like a ruler to measure the circumference of a circle because the boundary is curved.

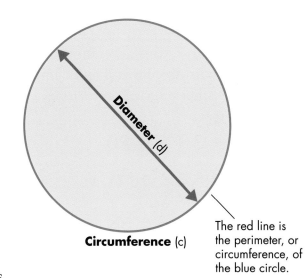

Diameter (d)

Circumference (c)

The red line is the perimeter, or circumference, of the blue circle.

Measuring the circumference

One way to measure the circumference is to roll the circle along a flat surface. You can try this out with a bicycle wheel.

Mark the tyre with chalk and then place the mark against a starting chalk-mark on the ground. Next, roll the wheel in a straight line until the mark meets the ground again. Mark this position on the ground.

Measure the distance between starting and finishing marks on the ground to get the length of the circumference.

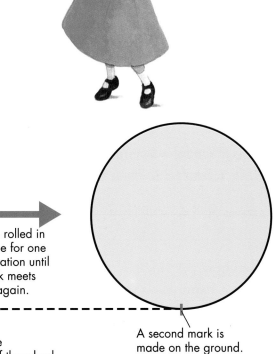

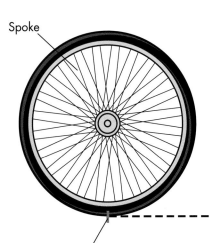

Spoke

Mark on tyre and ground.

The wheel is rolled in a straight line for one complete rotation until the tyre mark meets the ground again.

This length is the circumference of the wheel.

A second mark is made on the ground.

Calculating the circumference

Measuring the circumference of a circle is not easy, and so most people use a simple formula instead. The formula uses the diameter, the distance from one side of the circle to the other.
The formula is:

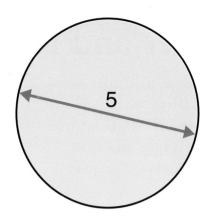

circumference (c) = **3.14 × diameter** (d)

It is common to use a small d for diameter and a small c for circumference, so the formula is then:

$$c = 3.14 \times d$$

So, for example, if the diameter of a circle is **5**, the circumference is:

$$c = 3.14 \times 5$$
$$c = 15.70$$

How to use a calculator
Step 1: Enter the diameter (5)
Step 2: Press multiplication sign (x)
Step 3: Enter 3.14
Step 4: Press equals sign (=)
(Answer 15.7)

Note: To find out why we use 3.14 in the formula, turn the page.

You can also use the radius of the circle. As the radius is half of the diameter, we need to replace the diameter by **2** times the radius in the formula. It is common to use a small r for radius, so the formula is then:

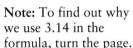

$$c = 3.14 \times 2 \times r$$

Word check
Circumference: The perimeter of a circle.

Diameter: The size of a circle measured straight across through its centre.

Formula: A rule for calculating something. It is often an equation containing a letter or several letters.

Radius: The distance from the centre of a circle to its boundary. It is half the diameter.

Remember... This formula can be used to find the circumference of a circle of any size.

Perimeter and roundness

All circles are the same shape: round. They are just different sizes. You may think this is obvious. But it isn't true for rectangles, triangles and most other common shapes.

The circumference (c) of a circle is always the diameter (d) multiplied by the same number. The Greeks were the first people to discover this fact and they called the number pi (π), the Greek for p, the first letter of periphery, which is another word for circumference.

$$\pi = \frac{22}{7} \text{ or } 3.14$$

pi (π) is approximately 3.14 or $\frac{22}{7}$

As a result you can use either of these formulae:

circumference (c) = **3.14** × **diameter** (d)

or

circumference (c) = $\frac{22}{7}$ × **diameter** (d)

Fenced off

Harvey wanted to put a fence around his garden pond to stop his dog from jumping in it. His pond was 7 metres across. How much fencing did he need?

We know that the circumference of a circle is found by using the formula:

$$c = \frac{22}{7} \times d$$

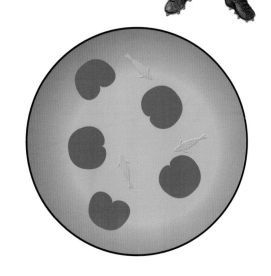

This time we have chosen the formula that includes a fraction.

Putting the pond diameter into the formula gives:

$$c = \frac{22}{7} \times 7$$

dividing through by 7:

$$c = 22 \text{ m}$$

The drum

John wanted to buy enough cord to go exactly around a replica African drum he was making. The cord would be stuck to the drum to make a fine finishing edge.

John designed his drum to be **30** cm across, so he needed to calculate the circumference of the drum to find out how much cord to buy.

This time we will use the version of formula that includes the decimal number for pi.

Using the formula:

$$c = 3.14 \times d$$

$$c = 3.14 \times 30$$

$$c = 94.20 \text{ cm}$$

This is almost **100** cm or **1** metre, and so John needed to buy **1** metre of cord for each loop around the drum.

Remember… You can use either the decimal number or the fraction for pi in the formula. Use the one that you think will work out most easily.

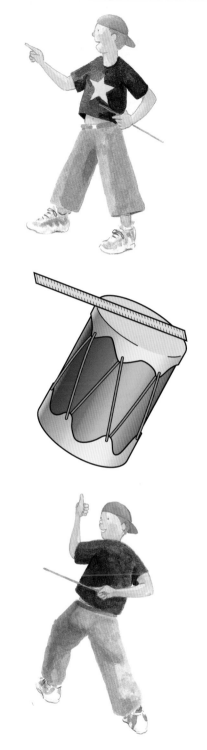

Word check

Periphery: Another word for circumference.

Pi: The number of times the circumference of a circle is bigger than the diameter. It is given a special name because it cannot be written down precisely as a fraction, or as a decimal. It is approximately $\frac{22}{7}$ or 3.14159265…

Length of mixed shapes

Many objects are made of straight and round sections. To find the combined length, deal with each type of shape separately, then add the results.

You can see how to do this using the example of a paper clip. A paper clip is made of a single piece of wire bent into round and straight parts

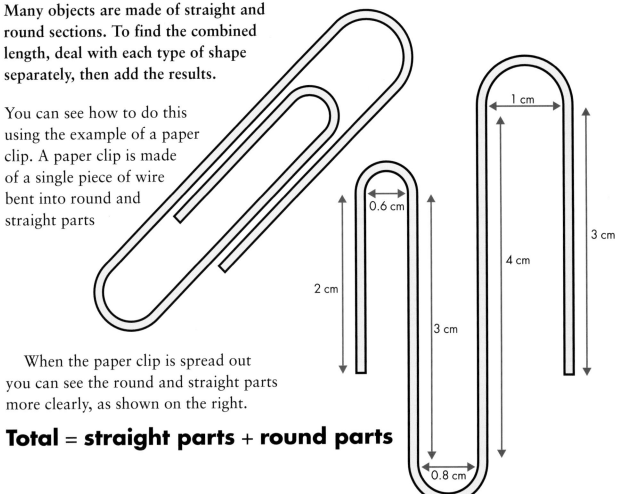

When the paper clip is spread out you can see the round and straight parts more clearly, as shown on the right.

Total = straight parts + round parts

Step 1: Start with the straight parts. There are four straight parts. Adding them we get:

$$3 + 4 + 2 + 3 = 12$$

Step 2: Next do the round parts. There are three round ends. Each round end is a semicircle – half a circle.

The width of the round end is the same as the diameter. Find the length of the larger round end.

This part is a semicircle. It is the same as half a circle. It makes up the round ends of the paperclip.

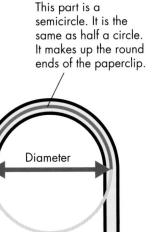

Diameter

The circumference of a circle is 3.14 × diameter. The round end is half a circle, so its length is:

$$\frac{3.14 \times \text{diameter}}{2}$$

We have three round ends. They have diameters of 1 centimetre, 0.8 centimetres and 0.6 centimetres. We put each of these diameters into the formula above like this:

1 cm diameter round end:

$$\frac{3.14 \times 1}{2} = 1.57$$

0.8 cm diameter round end:

$$\frac{3.14 \times 0.8}{2} = 1.26$$

0.6 cm diameter round end:

$$\frac{3.14 \times 0.6}{2} = 0.94$$

Adding these values gives us the length of the rounded parts:

$$1.57 + 1.26 + 0.94 = 3.77$$

Step 3: The total length of the paper clip is:

$$= 12 + 3.77$$
$$= 15.77 \text{ cm} \text{ (nearly 16 cm)}$$

Remember... If you want to find the length of a complicated shape, try to split up your task into easy parts such as straight sections and curved sections.

Book link... For more information on multiplying with decimals see the books *Multiplying* and *Decimals* in the *Maths Matters!* set.

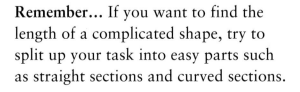

Areas of squares

The amount of surface something covers is called its area. Area is used to measure the size of the inside of a flat shape. It might be the amount of carpet you need to cover your bedroom floor, or the amount of turf needed to cover a lawn, or the amount of land covered by a forest, or country or state.

Unit squares and square units

When we measure area, we use square units. First, we draw a square which is one unit along each side. If we are measuring length in inches, the square will be 1 inch on each side. The area of that square is called 1 square inch, often written as 1 in^2.

If we are measuring length in centimetres, the square will be 1 cm on each side. The area of that square is called 1 square cm, often written as 1 cm^2.

Calculating areas of squares

To find the area of a square, use this formula:

area (a) = **length** (ℓ) × **width** (w)

$$a = \ell \times w$$

Because every side in a square is the same length, the area is simply any side multiplied by itself.

Finding areas of squares

Each playing square on the chess board in the picture opposite has a side **5 cm** long. We can find the area of one playing square by counting how many 1 cm² squares can be fitted into it.

You can see from the diagram below that **25** of these fit in. We say that the area of the playing square is **25 cm²**.

8 squares

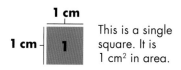

1 cm

1 cm

This is a single square. It is 1 cm² in area.

5 cm

5 cm

Each square has a side of 5 cm

Alternatively, we could have found the area by multiplying one side by itself:

$$a = 5 \times 5$$

$$a = 25 \text{ cm}^2$$

which, of course, is far quicker.

Remember... Because a square has sides all the same length, the area is found by multiplying the length of any side by itself.

Word check

Area: The size of the shape within a boundary. It is measured in square units by counting how many unit squares can be fitted into it.

Square unit: The same area as is in a square with sides one unit long. It can be any shape.

Areas of rectangles

A rectangle is a shape with four straight sides, and corners that are all right angles. Unlike a square, the touching sides are not the same length.

You can see the difference between a square and a rectangle by looking again at the chess board.

'My half' of the chess board is the four rows at my end. Each row contains eight playing squares. 'My half' is a rectangle.

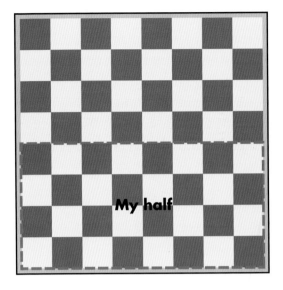

The area of a rectangle is found by the formula:

$$\textbf{area } (a) = \textbf{length } (\ell) \times \textbf{width } (w)$$

$$a = \ell \times w$$

The 4 rows total 20 cm, the 8 columns total 40 cm.

So the area is:

$$a = 20 \times 40$$

$$a = 800 \text{ cm}^2$$

Check your calculation

You can count that I have **32** playing squares in my half of the board. Each one is 5 cm × 5 cm or **25 cm²**.

You can multiply the number of playing squares by the area of each one:

$$a = 32 \times 25$$

$$a = 800 \text{ cm}^2$$

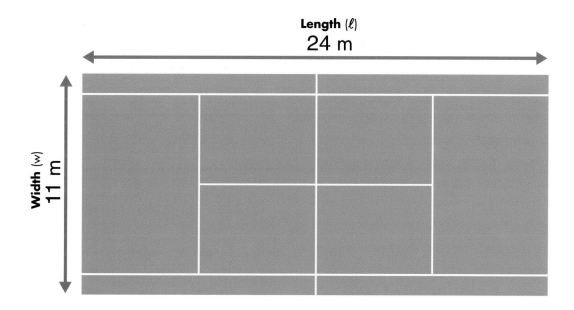

Length (ℓ)
24 m

Width (w)
11 m

The area of a tennis court

A tennis court is **24** metres long and **11** metres wide.

To find its area, we could cover it with squares 1 metre on each side, and count them.

Or we could add **24 + 24 + 24 +** etc., eleven times (or add **11 + 11 + 11 +** etc., twenty-four times) or we could multiply **24 × 11**, which is by far the quickest method.

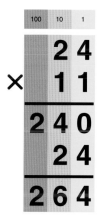

100	10	1
	2	**4**
×	**1**	**1**
2	**4**	**0**
	2	**4**
2	**6**	**4**

The answer is **264** m².

Book link... To find out more about multiplication using columns, see the book *Multiplying* in the *Maths Matters!* set

Remember... Multiplying is a quick way of adding similar things, which is what we are doing when we count areas.

Word Check

Rectangle: A four-sided shape in which pairs of opposite sides are the same length and all four corners are right angles.

Right angle: An angle which is exactly a quarter of a complete turn.

Areas of triangles

One way to think of the area of a triangle is to imagine it as half a rectangle. To understand how to find the area of a triangle, start with a rectangle, like the one to the right, and draw a line between opposite corners (a diagonal).

Both parts of the rectangle are now triangles, and as both are the same shape and size, you can see that the area of one triangle is half the area of the rectangle. On page 18 we saw that the area of a rectangle (a) is length (ℓ) multiplied by width (w):

$$a = \ell \times w$$

and as the area of a triangle is half of this, the area of a triangle is:

$$a = \frac{1}{2}\ell \times w$$

When dealing with triangles, mathematicians normally use the word 'base' for the horizontal side and 'height' for the line at right angles to the base.

This means that we write the area as:

$$a = \frac{1}{2}b \times h$$

This formula is always true, no matter what shape the triangle.

See how the height divides the rectangle into two pairs of equal triangles, showing that the area of any triangle is half the area of the rectangle.

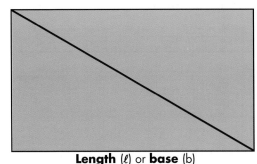

Width (w)
or
height (h)

Length (ℓ) or **base** (b)

The shaded part of each rectangle has the same area as the unshaded part.

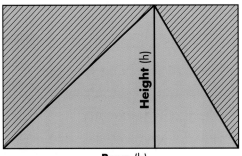

Height (h)

Base (b)

Areas of triangles with the same base and height are always the same

Two gardeners were arguing over the biggest area of a triangular flower bed. One side had to be the same length as a window and the flower bed also had to reach to the path. The first gardener said that his broad triangle would have the biggest area, while the second said that a triangle with the longest possible sides would have a bigger area.

Who was right? They were both wrong because the area of a triangle is ½ base × height, as we saw on page 22. The base for both triangles is the window, and as they must also both reach the path, the height of the triangles will also be the same. So, no matter what shape of triangle they laid out, the area would always be the same.

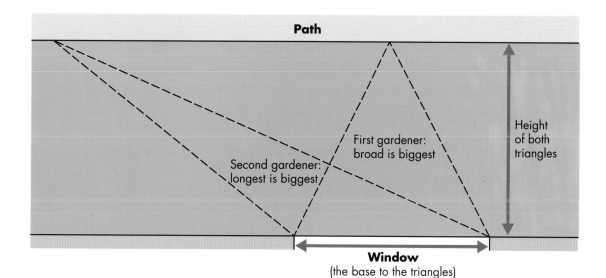

Path

First gardener: broad is biggest

Second gardener: longest is biggest

Height of both triangles

Window
(the base to the triangles)

Remember... The formula:
area of triangle (a) = ½ base (b) × height (h).
The height of a triangle is always measured perpendicularly to the base.

Word Check

Base: The starting line for drawing a triangle.

Parallel: Parallel lines are lines which will remain the same distance apart for ever.

Perpendicular: Two lines which meet or cross at right angles are called perpendicular.

The difference between squares

Finding areas can often be done by both multiplication and subtraction.

A new garden

The chief gardener for the city council designed a new pattern of flower beds for the main square. The beds would be laid out using two squares, one inside the other, as shown. The centre square would be filled with flowering plants, while the outer triangles would be mountain plants growing in beds of gravel. The assistant gardener had to find out how much gravel was needed for the triangular beds. For this he needed to know the areas of the triangles.

   He tried to find the answer in two ways, as described below.

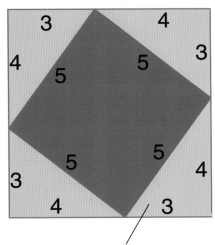

These triangular areas are to be covered with gravel.

Example 1

The design is made from two squares, one inside the other. The area of gravel can be seen as the difference between the areas of the squares:

Area of larger square (a) = length (ℓ) × width (w):

$$a = 7 \times 7 = 49$$

Area of smaller square (a) = length (ℓ) × width (w):

$$a = 5 \times 5 = 25$$

Difference in areas = larger square – smaller square:

$$49 - 25 = 24 \text{ m}^2$$

Book link... Find out more about how to work out the difference between two squares in the book *Mental Arithmetic* in the *Maths Matters!* set.

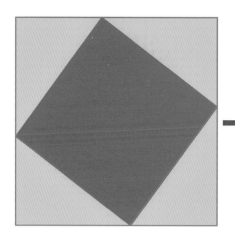

To see why you can subtract areas, the smaller shape has been turned around to show you that it is a simple square.

Example 2

Area of each of the triangles is:

$$a = \frac{1}{2}b \times h$$

$$a = \frac{1}{2} \times 3 \times 4$$

$$a = 6$$

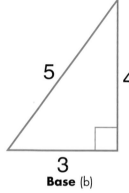

5

4 **Height** (h)

3
Base (b)

There are four identical triangles, so the total area of the triangles is:

$$a = 6 \times 4$$

$$a = 24 \text{ m}^2$$

The answer in both examples was 24 square metres (m²).

Remember... When you can use two ways to solve a problem, it is sensible to use both to check the answer.

Word Check

Parallel: Parallel lines are lines which will remain the same distance apart for ever.

Perpendicular: Two lines which meet or cross at right angles are called perpendicular.

Mixed rectangles and triangles

Many shapes are more complicated than simply rectangles, triangles or circles. These are mixed shapes.

To find the area of a mixed shape, draw lines to separate out the shapes into rectangles, triangles or circles.

Next, find the area of each part and finally add the parts together.

Here is an example.

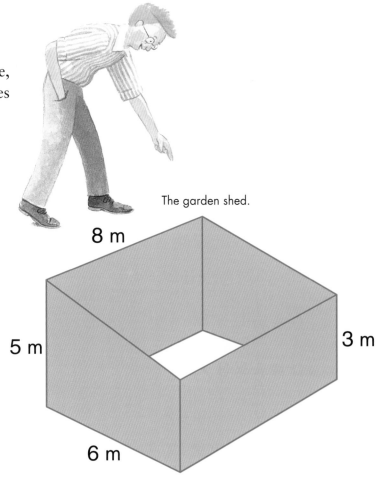

The garden shed.

Painting the garden shed

Tom's dad had to paint the walls of a large shed. To do this he needed to know the area of the outside of the shed so that he could order the right amount of paint.

We have three shapes in this problem. Let's start with the rectangles. At the back of the shed there is a deep rectangle. Using the formula:

$$\textbf{area (a)} = \textbf{length } (\ell) \times \textbf{width (w)}$$

the area of the back of the shed is:

$$a = 8 \times 5$$
$$a = 40$$

At the front there is a shallow rectangle:

$$a = 8 \times 3$$
$$a = 24$$

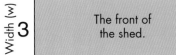

The sides are more complicated, but they can be simplified into a rectangle and a triangle. First the area of each rectangle is:

$$a = 6 \times 3$$

$$a = 18$$

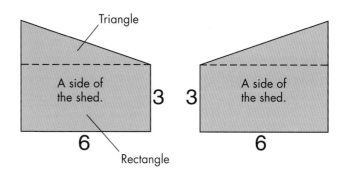

Triangle

A side of the shed.

3

3

A side of the shed.

6

6

Rectangle

Now the area of each triangle.

area (a) = half base (b) × height (h)

The base is 6. The height is the height of the back minus the front height or 5 − 3 = 2 , therefore:

$$a = \frac{1}{2} \times 6 \times 2$$

$$a = 6$$

Therefore the area of one side equals the area of the rectangle plus the area of the triangle:

$$a = 18 + 6$$

$$a = 24$$

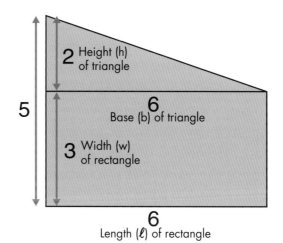

2   Height (h) of triangle

5

6
Base (b) of triangle

3   Width (w) of rectangle

6
Length (ℓ) of rectangle

Remember, there are two sides, so the area of the two sides is:

$$a = 24 \times 2 = 48$$

Adding sides to the ends gives:

$$a = 40 + 24 + 48$$

$$a = 112 \text{ m}^2$$

All the answers could be in square yards or whatever unit you are working with.

Remember… Split up complicated shapes into simpler shapes, then add the results.

Mixed circles and rectangles

The area of a circle can be found using the formula:

$$a = \pi r^2$$

(area is pi multiplied by the radius squared).

Or the formula:

$$a = \frac{\pi d^2}{4}$$

(area is pi multiplied by the diameter squared divided by 4).

Turfing a running track

The groundsman of a running track had to sow a specially hard-wearing new sports grass over the inside area of the track. He needed to work out the area inside the track so that he would know how much seed to order.

To find the area of a running track, split the calculation into two parts. First, calculate the area of the two semicircular ends (two semicircles make a circle). The diameter of the circle is 70 metres. So the easiest formula to use is the one with the diameter in it. In this case we will also choose to use the fraction value of ²²⁄₇ for pi.

$$a = \frac{22}{7} \times \frac{70 \times 70}{4}$$

Dividing through by 7:

$$a = \frac{22}{1} \times \frac{10 \times 70}{4}$$

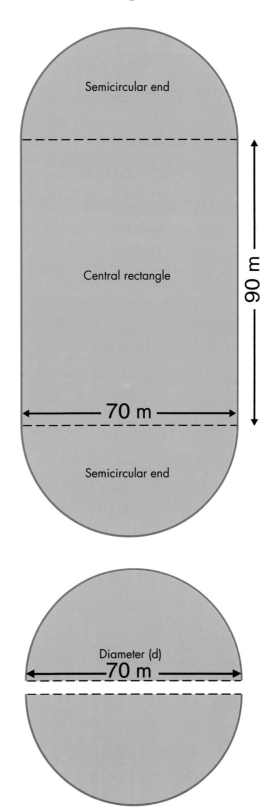

Semicircular end

Central rectangle

90 m

70 m

Semicircular end

Diameter (d)
70 m

Dividing through by 2:

$$a = \frac{11}{1} \times \frac{10 \times 70}{2}$$

Dividing through by 2 again:

$$a = 11 \times 5 \times 70$$

$$a = 3,850 \text{ m}^2$$

The area of the two semicircular ends together comes to 3,850 m².

The area of the central rectangle can easily be found using the formula for the area of a rectangle from page 20:

$$a = \ell \times w$$

The length (ℓ) is 90 m and the width (w) is 70 m, so the area is:

$$a = 90 \times 70$$

$$a = 6,300 \text{ m}^2$$

The groundsman will need enough seed to sow grass on the total area of:

$$a = 3,850 + 6,300$$

$$a = 10,150 \text{ m}^2$$

Remember... Formulas for areas have two length measurements multiplied together:
$a = \ell \times w$ (rectangle)
$a = \pi \times r \times r$ (circle)

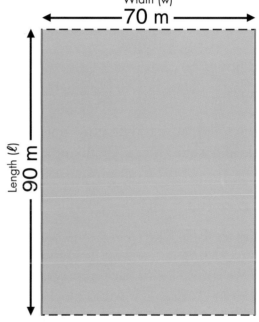

Width (w)
70 m

Length (ℓ)
90 m

Volumes of box shapes

The amount of space taken up by something is called its volume. It might be the amount of space in your lunch box, the amount of space in a freezer taken up by an ice-cream tub, or the amount of water in a lake or an ocean.

Volume measures the size of a three dimensional (3D) object, which has a thickness as well as length and width.

For volume, we use one cubic metre, 1 cubic foot or whatever unit we are interested in. It is written m^3, ft^3 and so on.

Calculating volume

This box is **50** centimetres long, **30** centimetres high and **40** centimetres wide.

Here is how to find the volume (v) of the box and, at the same time, find a formula for the volume of any object.

The area of the front of the box is:

$$a = 50 \times 30$$
$$a = 1{,}500 \text{ cm}^2$$

If we travel 1 unit back along the width, we could stack **1,500** blocks each 1 cm × 1 cm × 1 cm.

By the time we reach the back of the box, we could have done this **40** times.

So the amount of space taken up by the box is:

$$v = 1{,}500 \times 40$$
$$v = 60{,}000 \text{ cm}^3$$

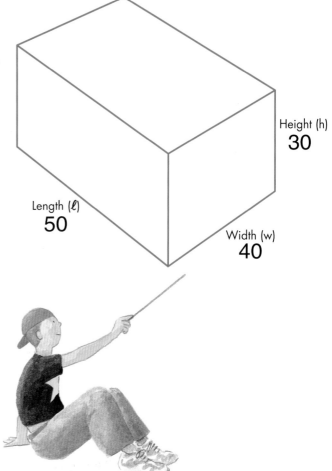

Height (h)
30

Length (ℓ)
50

Width (w)
40

Therefore, the formula for volume (v) is:

volume (v) = **width** (w) × **height** (h) × **length** (ℓ)

Finding the capacity of a freezer

The maximum volume that something can hold is called its capacity. The inside space of a freezer is 70 cm high, 70 cm deep and 170 cm wide. How much can it hold?

The capacity is:

$$v = \ell \times w \times h$$

$$v = 170 \times 70 \times 70$$

$$v = 833{,}000 \text{ cm}^3$$

There are 1,000 cm³ in 1 litre, so the capacity of the material that could be fitted inside is 833 litres.

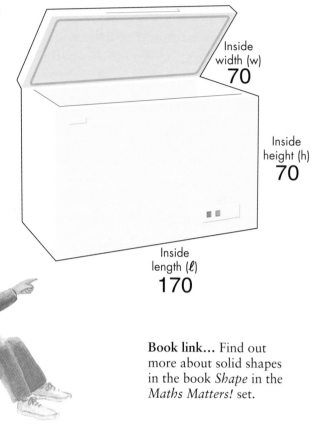

Inside width (w)
70

Inside height (h)
70

Inside length (ℓ)
170

Book link... Find out more about solid shapes in the book *Shape* in the *Maths Matters!* set.

Remember... The formula for finding a volume (v) is:
volume = length × width × depth.

Word check

3D: A three-dimensional shape (3D) has length and breadth and thickness (depth). It can be solid, just a surface, or even an open framework, like a pylon.

Capacity: The maximum volume that a container can hold. It is measured in special units such as pints or litres.

Cubic unit: The same volume as is contained in a unit cube. It can be any shape.

Cuboid: A 3D shape with six faces that are all rectangles; some but not all may be squares.

Volume: The size of a 3D shape. It is measured in cubic units (such as cm³ or in³) by counting how many unit cubes can be fitted into it.

Volumes of other solid shapes

The volume of cans and some other containers can be found in the same way as for a box.

Volume of a cylinder or rod

There are many cylinders in your kitchen used as containers for honey, cocoa and other things.

The formula to use for the volume is:

$$\textbf{volume = area of end} \times \textbf{length}$$

Area of circular end:

$$a = \frac{\pi d^2}{4} \quad \text{(see page 28)}$$

$$a = \frac{22}{7} \times \frac{14 \times 14}{4}$$

Dividing through by 7:

$$a = \frac{22}{1} \times \frac{2 \times 14}{4}$$

Dividing through by 2:

$$a = 11 \times 1 \times 14$$

$$a = 154 \text{ cm}^2$$

The volume is area of end × length:

$$v = 154 \times 20$$

$$v = 3{,}080 \text{ cm}^2$$

As **1** litre is **1,000** cm³, this is just over **3** litres.

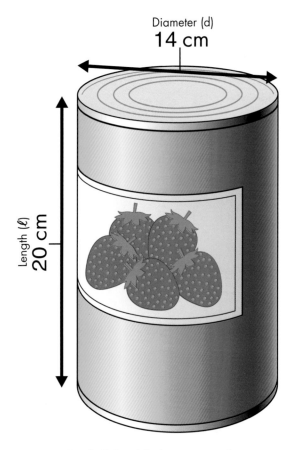

Diameter (d)
14 cm

Length (ℓ)
20 cm

Book link... Find out more about cylinders and other shapes in the book *Shape* in the *Maths Matters!* set.

Volume of a pyramid

The volume of a pyramid is exactly a third of the volume of a box that it will just fit into.

In this diagram the height of the box is the same as the height of the pyramid, while the base of the box is the same as the base of the pyramid.

The formula is:

$$\textbf{volume} = \frac{1}{3} \textbf{ of the area of the base} \times \textbf{height}$$

The volume of a giant pyramid

The largest of the pyramids at Giza, Egypt, is called Khufu's pyramid. It is one of the greatest man-made wonders of the ancient world. About one hundred thousand people working part-time may have built the pyramid over 20 years.

The sides of its base are **230** m (**755** ft) long and it originally reached **147** m (**481** ft) in height.

The volume of the pyramid is:

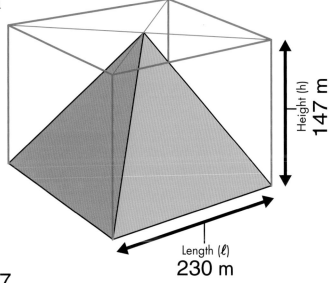

Height (h)
147 m

Length (ℓ)
230 m

$$v = \frac{1}{3} \times 230 \times 230 \times 147$$

$$v = 2{,}592{,}100 \text{ cubic metres}$$

(The stones to make it weighed nearly **6** million tonnes in total!)

Remember... Volume of a cylinder is: area of end × height.

The volume of any pyramid is ⅓ the volume of the box that it will just fit into.

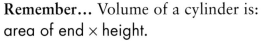

Angles

A degree is the unit of angle, or turn. The ancient Babylonians invented the use of degrees because they found **60** a very easy number to work with. The Babylonians used a triangle with three equal sides (an equilateral triangle), and divided each of the angles into **60** equal parts. Each of these little angles is called one degree.

If you add **360** degrees together, you make a complete turn.

360 is a very convenient number of degrees to have in a full circle. **360** divides by all of these numbers:

2, 3, 4, 5, 6, 8, 9, 10, 12, 15, 18, 20, 24, 30, 36, 40, 45, 60, 72, 90, 120 and 180.

Dividing a whole turn into equal parts using any of these numbers will produce a whole number of degrees for an answer.

Some common angles are:

A quarter turn, or right angle, is 90 degrees.

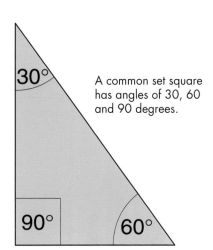

A common set square has angles of 30, 60 and 90 degrees.

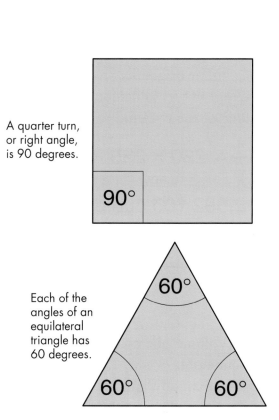

Each of the angles of an equilateral triangle has 60 degrees.

Angles are measured with an instrument called a protractor, a measuring instrument marked off in degrees. It can be used to measure, or to draw angles.

There are three main types of protractor. The most common is a semicircular protractor, which has a flat base. It has a centre point, and its flat base is parallel to a line called a zero line. There are two scales so that you can measure an angle either from the left or the right. Each scale goes from 0 to 180°.

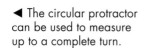
◄ A semicircular protractor

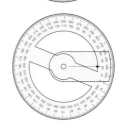
◄ The circular protractor can be used to measure up to a complete turn.

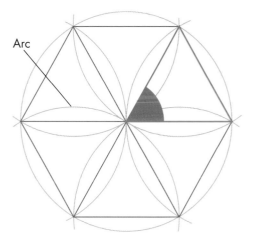
◄ The third type of protractor is called an angle measurer. This is a circular protractor with a moveable arm. To measure an angle with a protractor, line up the zero line along one arm of the angle with the point of the angle at the centre of the protractor. Then read the angle on the scale.

Triangles that do a complete turn

Circles, triangles and the amount of turning are all closely related in a natural way. The natural way to divide a circle is like this:

Draw a circle using a pair of compasses. Without changing the separation on your compasses, put the point anywhere on the boundary, draw an arc, move the point of the compasses to where the arc crosses the circle boundary, and draw another arc. Repeat until you come back to your starting point.

Arc

The red triangle is an equilateral triangle, because using your compasses, you made all of its sides the same length. Six of these equilateral triangles make up a whole turn. The angle shaded red between the two red arms is exactly one-sixth of a whole turn. A whole turn is 360° and so a sixth of a turn is 60°. Thus 60 is a natural unit to choose for measuring the amount of turn.

Book link... Find out more about numbers in the book *Numbers* in the *Maths Matters!* set.

Remember... Although you can divide a complete turn into 360 degrees, the most useful angles to remember are 30°, 60° and 90°.

Word check
Arc: Part of a circle. It is drawn using compasses.

Degree: A small part of a complete turn. There are 360 degrees in a complete turn. It is shown by the symbol °.

How to divide an angle in half

Dividing an angle in half can be done
easily with a pair of compasses.

Step 1: Draw the angle you want to divide.

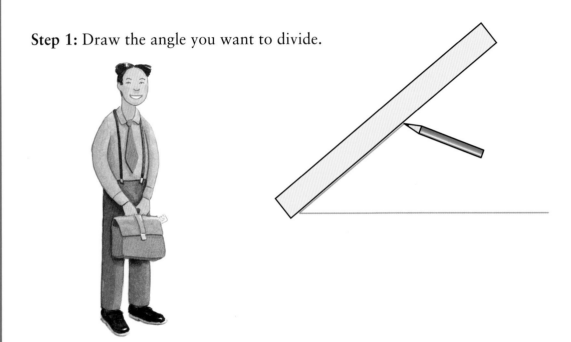

Step 2: Open your compasses to
any convenient width and draw an
arc from the point of the angle O.

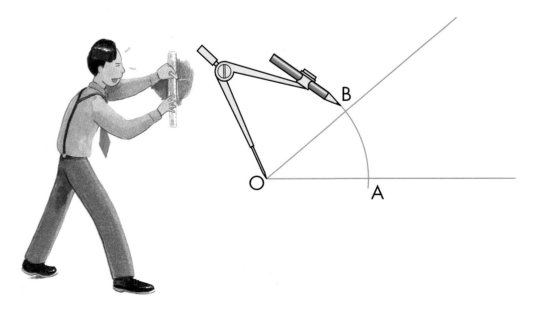

Step 3: Keeping the compasses the same width, use points A and B to place the point of your compasses. From each point draw another arc.

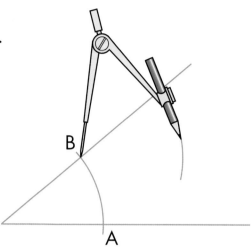

When you have done this, you will find that the arcs cross. On our diagram we have marked this point of crossing as M.

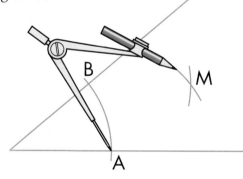

Step 4: If you join point O to point M you will have a line that divides the angle in two exactly.

The angles of a triangle add up to 180°

One of the most important properties of triangles is that the angles of a triangle add up to **180°**, which is half a complete turn or a straight angle. You can see this by using three identical triangles. In this case we are using a **30–60–90** triangle, but <u>any</u> identical triangles can be used.

Step 1: Place one triangle on a line drawn on a piece of paper.

30°

90°   60°

This base line is a straight angle or 180°.

Step 2: Place the second triangle so that the **30°** angle lines up with the **90°** angle of the first triangle.

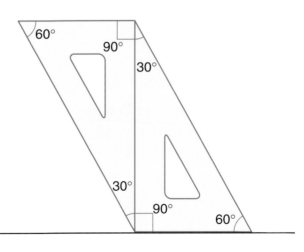

60°

90°

30°

30°

90°   60°

Step 3: Now place the third set square so that the 60° angle lines up next to the 30° and the 90° angles.

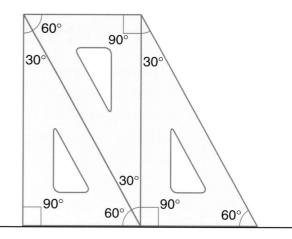

When you put the last set square in place, the edge of the set square lies along the base line, showing that three angles of a triangle add up to half a turn:

$$90° + 30° + 60° = 180°$$

Below is a triangle cut from cardboard. There is nothing special about the angles. Each corner has been cut off and rearranged on a base line. Again they make half a turn, or 180°.

Book link... Find out more about triangles in the book *Shape* in the *Maths Matters!* set.

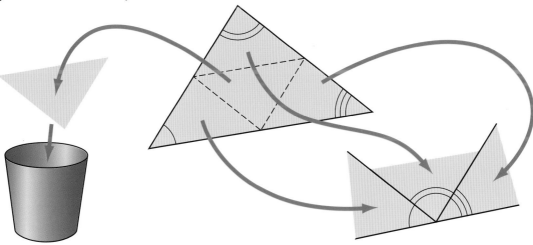

Remember... Triangles come in many shapes. The three angles <u>always</u> total 180°.

Finding the missing angle

The fact that the three inside angles of a triangle add up to **180°** can be used to find the value of a missing angle when two others are known.

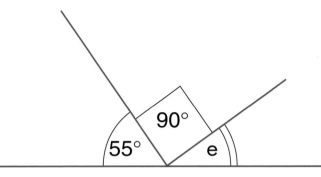

In the diagram on the right you can see that three lines have been drawn so that three angles are formed. Two of the angles are known, but we need to find the size of the third angle.

We know that a half turn is **180°**. So all the angles must add up to 180°:

$$55° + 90° + e = 180°$$

Because:

$$55° + 90° = 145°$$

So:

$$145° + e = 180°$$

Now, take **145** from each side of the equation:

$$e = 180° - 145°$$

$$e = 35°$$

Here is another example. Find m:

$$57° + 47° + m = 180°$$

$$104° + m = 180°$$

Take 104 from both sides:

$$m = 76°$$

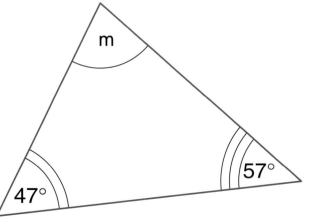

In this example you have been given only one angle. However, the triangle has two equal angles because it is an isosceles triangle. So the other base angle must also be 70°:

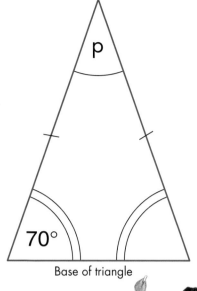

$$70° + 70° + p = 180°$$
$$140° + p = 180°$$

Take 140° from both sides of the equation:

$$p = 40°$$

Base of triangle

Here is another isosceles triangle. In this case we are given the unequal angle, and we know that the other two angles are the same.

$$2 \times q + 128° = 180°$$

Take 128° from each side of the equation:

$$2 \times q = 52°$$

Now divide each side by 2:

$$q = \frac{52°}{2}$$
$$q = 26°$$

Base of triangle

(Check: 26° + 26° + 128° = 180°)

Remember... Always check your answer by adding the three angles together. They must come to 180°.

Word check
Isosceles: A triangle or a trapezium with just two sides the same length is called isosceles.

Enlargement

When you enlarge something you change its size, not its shape, or its angles.

By enlarging an object, all of its lengths are multiplied by the same number.

When you enlarge something, you multiply all of its lengths by a number bigger than 1. If you multiply its lengths by a number smaller than 1 you make it smaller. This is called reducing. Reducing and enlarging are therefore opposites.

This green triangle is an enlargement of the blue triangle. It is also an enlargement of the red triangle.

This red triangle is a reduction of both the blue and the green triangles.

This blue triangle is an enlargement of the red triangle. It is also a reduction of the green triangle.

Drawing an enlargement

The easiest way to enlarge or reduce something is often to make a scale drawing of it.

Decide by how much you want to enlarge the object. In this case we are going to make a square 2 times bigger, as shown on page 43.

Step 1: Use a piece of graph paper and draw out the square close to the bottom left of it.

Mark a position in the bottom left-hand corner of the paper. This will be the centre from which we make our enlargement.

Draw a ray (a line) from your centre of enlargement through all four corners of the square.

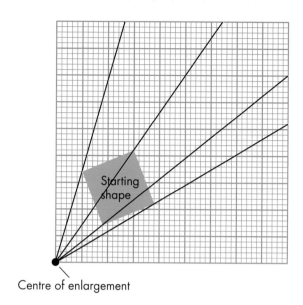

Centre of enlargement

Step 2: Select one ray, and measure the distance from the centre of enlargement to the corner of the square. Now multiply this distance by **2** and mark a second point along the ray where this comes.

Measure this distance

Mark out this distance to be twice as long

A corner of the enlarged square

Step 3: Repeat step 2 for all four corners, and mark points twice as far along each ray as the distance from the centre to each corner.

Join the four new points to show the enlarged square.

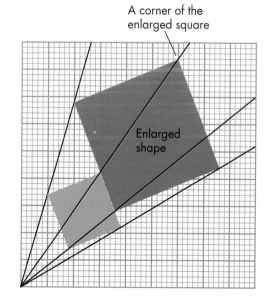

Enlarged shape

Remember... The easiest way to make a shape bigger or smaller is to use the drawing method.

What symbols mean

Some common geometry symbols together with an example of how they are used:

Right angle (90°)

Curves in angles show that the angle is larger than, or less than, a right angle.

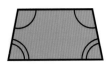

Angles with the same number of curves are the same size.

Outer line: The boundary of a shape.

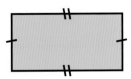

Ticks: Lines (sides or diagonals) with the same number of ticks are the same length.

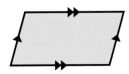

Arrowheads: Sides with the same number of arrowheads are parallel.

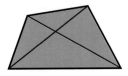

Diagonal lines: A line crossing the inside of a shape from one corner to another.

Dashed lines show lines of flip symmetry.

Some common maths symbols:

+ The symbol for adding. We say it 'plus'. In Latin *plus* means 'more'.

— Between two numbers this symbol means 'subtract' or 'minus'. In front of one number it means the number is a minus number. In Latin *minus* means 'less'.

✗ The symbol for multiplying. We say it 'multiplied by' or 'times'.

—, **/** and **÷** Three symbols for dividing. We say it 'divided by'. A pair of numbers above and below a / or — make a fraction, so ²⁄₅ or $\frac{2}{5}$ is the fraction two-fifths.

= The symbol for equals. We say it 'equals' or 'makes'. It comes from a Latin word meaning 'level' because weighing scales are level when the amounts on each side are equal.

■ This is a decimal point. It is a dot written after the units when a number contains parts of a unit as well as whole numbers.

( ) The symbols for brackets. You do everything inside the brackets first. Brackets always occur in pairs.

% : The symbol for per cent.

π : The symbol for pi.

° : The symbol for degrees.

Glossary

This glossary contains the Word check items from earlier in the book along with many other terms commonly used in mathematics.

Acute angle: An angle that is smaller than a right angle.

Adding: A quick way of counting.

Arc: Part of a circle. It is drawn using compasses.

Area: The size of the shape within a boundary. It is measured in square units by counting how many unit squares can be fitted into it.

Base: The starting line for drawing a triangle.

Bisect: To cut exactly in half.

Boundary: The line or curve separating the inside of the shape you are interested in from everything outside it.

Capacity: The maximum volume that a container can hold. It is measured in special units such as pints or litres.

Chart: A diagram used to show data from tables. There are many kinds of charts, including bar charts and pie charts. *See* Graph.

Circle: A loop whose boundary is the same distance from the centre all the way round.

Circumference: The perimeter of a circle. In Latin *circum* means 'around' and '-ference' comes from a word meaning 'carrying'.

Column: Things placed one below the other. In a table the entries which are in a line that goes up and down the page.

Compasses: An instrument for drawing circles and arcs. It has two arms jointed at the top. One arm has a pin for the centre of the circle. The other arm has a pencil or pen to draw the circle.

Cone: A pyramid with a circle for a base. It may be solid or surface.

Corner: A place where two lines meet. A square has four corners, each made where neighbouring sides meet. The word corner is also often used for triangles. *See* Vertex.

Cube: A 3D shape in which all six faces are squares.

Cubic unit: The same volume as is contained in a unit cube. It can be any shape.

Cuboid: A 3D shape with six faces that are all rectangles; some but not all may be squares.

Cylinder: A 3D shape that can be made by, for example, rolling up a piece of paper. It may be solid – in which case it is a rod – or may be hollow.

Data: Information from which you start to solve a problem. You might have collected it yourself or have been given it. The word comes from Latin meaning 'things given'.

Decimal number: A number that contains parts of units as well as whole units. The decimal point is used to separate the units from the parts of a unit.

Decimal place: The digits used for parts of a unit, such as tenths and hundredths. For example, if a number is given to '2 decimal places', it means that there are digits in the tenths and hundredths columns.

Decimal point: A dot written after the units when a number contains parts of a unit as well as whole numbers.

Degree: A small part of a complete turn. There are 360 degrees in a complete turn.

Diagonal: A line crossing the inside of a shape from one corner to another.

Diameter: The size of a circle measured straight across through its centre. In Greek, *dia* means 'through' and *metria* means 'measurement'.

Digit: The numerals 1, 2, 3, 4, 5, 6, 7, 8, 9 or 0. Several may be used to stand for a larger number. They are called digits to make it clear that they are only part of a complete number. So we might say, "The second digit is 4", meaning the second numeral from the left. Or we might say, "That is a two-digit number", meaning that it has two numerals in it, tens and units.

Disc: A solid cylinder whose thickness is much less than its diameter.

Dividing: A quick way of separating a number into many equal parts.

Dividing line: The line that separates the two number parts of a fraction. It is sometimes written horizontally, — and sometimes sloping, / . It is also called the division line. It is one of the signs mathematicians use for dividing. The other is ÷.

Edge: The line formed where two faces of an object meet.

Equals: The things on either side of an equals sign are the same.

Equation: A number sentence using the = symbol, telling us that two different ways of writing a number are the same. For example, 2 + 2 = 4 and 9 − 5 = 4.

Equilateral triangle: A triangle with sides of equal length and angles of equal size. It is the regular triangle.

Even number: A multiple of 2.

Exterior angle: The angle that is 180° minus the interior angle. The interior and exterior angle at a point thus make a straight angle. *See* Outside angle and Interior angle.

External angle: The larger angle at a corner. For example, the exterior angle at a corner of a rectangle is 270°; the interior angle is 90°. *See* Outside angle and Interior angle.

Face: A 2D flat (not curved) surface of a solid.

Flip symmetry: A shape which can be flipped over so that it looks just the same.

Formula: A rule for calculating something. It is often an equation containing a letter or several letters.

Fraction: A special form of division using a numerator and denominator. The line between the two is called a dividing line.

Graph: A diagram with two axes on which points are plotted and then joined by lines. *See* Chart.

Grid: A pattern of lines that cross at right angles that is used to make it easier to set out your work.

Hexagon: A 2D shape with six angles.

Horizontal: Level and flat, like the surface of still water.

Inside angle: The smaller angle between the lines at a corner. For example, the inside angle at a corner of a rectangle is 90°, the outside angle is 270°. *See* Interior angle, Exterior angle, External angle and Outside angle.

Intercept: The point where a line graph crosses the y-axis. It is the amount the line is lifted above a parallel line through the origin.

Internal (interior) angle: The smaller angle made where two lines meet. *See* Exterior angle, External angle and Inside angle.

Isosceles: A triangle or a trapezium with just two sides the same length is called isosceles.

Kite: A four-sided shape with two pairs of touching sides the same length, which looks like a traditional kite.

Line: A continuous mark made on a surface. It may be straight or curved, and it can go on for ever in both directions.

Line graph: A graph where a line is drawn through a set of points.

Loop: A line that is closed back on itself.

Map: A scale drawing of a place.

Minus: Another word meaning 'subtract'.

Minus numbers: The numbers which fall below zero on a number line (scale). Minus numbers or zero cannot be used for counting, only for measuring things like temperature. Minus numbers are also called negative numbers.

Multiple: A number of objects which can be rearranged into several rows of equal length and longer than just one.

Number: One or more numerals placed together represent the size of something (e.g. 45 is the numerals four and five placed together to represent the number forty-five).

Obtuse angle: An angle which is larger than a right angle and smaller than a straight angle.

Octagon: A 2D shape with eight angles.

Odd number: A number that cannot be divided by 2.

One-digit number: A number between 1 and 9.

Operation: A mathematical word for one of the key methods: adding, subtracting, multiplying and dividing.

Ordered numbers: Numbers used for putting things in order, such as first, second, third, fourth, fifth and so on. Also called 'ordinal numbers'. *See* Unordered numbers.

Outside angle: The angle at a point measured outside the shape it belongs to. *See* Exterior angle, External angle, Inside angle, Interior angle.

Oval: An egg-shaped loop (from the Latin word *ovum*, meaning 'egg'). An oval is usually formed by stretching a circle one way.

Pair: Two things which match up in some way.

Parallel: Parallel lines are lines which will remain the same distance apart for ever.

Parallelogram: A four-sided shape in which opposite sides are parallel.

Pentagon: A 2D shape with five angles.

Per cent: A number followed by the % symbol means the number is divided by 100. It is a way of writing a fraction.

Perimeter: The size of the boundary of a flat object. It is the distance once around it. In Greek *peri* means 'around' and *metria* means 'measurement'.

Periphery: Another word for circumference.

Perpendicular: Two lines which meet or cross at right angles are called perpendicular.

Pi: The number of times the circumference of a circle is bigger than the diameter. It is given a special name because it cannot be written down precisely as a fraction or as a decimal. It is approximately ²²⁄₇ or **3.14159265....**

Plus numbers: The numbers which come above zero on a number line (scale). They are called this to separate them clearly from minus numbers. They are the same as counting numbers. Plus numbers are also called positive numbers.

Polyhedron: A general word for an entirely straight-edged 3D shape.

Powers: Little symbols written above the line, like the 4 in 10^4. 10^4 is said 'ten to the fourth' and means 1 followed by 4 zeros, which is $10 \times 10 \times 10 \times 10$. Powers are sometimes called exponents or indices.

Prime number: A number which is not a multiple of anything (2, 3, 5, 7, 11, 13, 17, 19 etc., are prime numbers).

Prism: A 3D shape made by building a 2D shape up from the paper so that it gains thickness, keeping the size and shape of the 2D shape the same. A rod is a prism made by pulling a disc into a 3D shape.

Protractor: A circular or semicircular instrument for measuring angles.

Quadrilateral: An entirely straight-sided 2D shape with only four corners.

Radius: The distance from the centre of a circle to its boundary. It is half the diameter. In Latin *radius* means a 'ray' or 'wheel spoke'.

Ratio: A method of comparing different numbers by placing them on either side of a colon (:); for example 1:2. The numbers must be measured in the same units. The order of the numbers matters. A ratio is like a fraction.

Ray: A straight line that starts from a point and goes straight on for ever in one direction only.

Rectangle: A four-sided shape in which pairs of opposite sides are the same length and all four corners are right angles.

Reflection: A 'mirror image' of a shape.

Rhombus: A four-sided shape with two pairs of parallel sides and all four sides the same length.

Right angle: An angle which is exactly a quarter of a complete turn.

Rod: A solid cylinder which has a length much greater than its diameter.

Rotation: Another word for turn.

Row: Things placed side by side. In a table the entries which are in any line across the page.

Scale: A set of marks on a line used for measuring.

Sector: A piece of a circle, like a piece of a pie.

Semicircle: Half a circle. In Latin *semi* means 'half'.

Set: A collection of things we are interested in.

Single-digit number: A number between 0 and 9.

Slope: A surface or line which is not level. How much (or steeply) it goes up is measured by the ratio UP:ACROSS.

Solid: A 3D object that is completely filled in, i.e. not hollow.

Sphere: A 3D shape made by spinning a circle around a diameter. It may be solid or just a surface.

Square: A regular rectangle with all four sides the same length and four angles of equal size.

Square root: The number which, multiplied by itself, produces a square number.

Square unit: The same area as is in a square with sides one unit long. It can be any shape.

Stepping stones: Easy numbers used to simplify finding your way through a calculation you are doing in your head.

Straight angle: An angle that is exactly half a turn.

Subtracting: A quick way of counting back to find out how many are left after you remove some.

Sum: The result of adding two or more numbers. *See* Total.

Surface: The outside of an object.

Symbol: A mark written on paper or something else to stand for a letter, a number or an idea of any kind.

Symmetry: The property of a shape that allows it to be turned about a point or flipped over a line and still look just the same.

Table: An arrangement of rows and columns for sorting and storing data.

Terminating decimal: An exact decimal. *See* Recurring decimal.

Tetrahedron: A 3D shape with four faces, all triangles (from the Greek *tetra*, meaning 'four').

Three-digit number: A number between 100 and 999.

Three-dimensional (3D): A three-dimensional shape (3D) has length and breadth and thickness (depth). It can be solid, just a surface, or even an open framework, like a pylon.

Total: The answer to an adding problem. *See* Sum.

Trapezium: A four-sided 2D shape with one pair of parallel sides.

Triangle: A straight-sided 2D shape with only three corners.

Turn: Another word for angle. A quarter of a turn is 90°, a half turn is 180°, a full turn is 360°.

Two-digit number: A number between 10 and 99.

Two-dimensional (2D): A two-dimensional shape (2D) has length and breadth but no thickness. Drawings on paper are 2D.

Unit cube: A cube whose sides are one unit (metre, foot, mile etc.) long. Its volume is one cubic unit.

Unit square: A square whose sides are one unit (metre, foot, mile etc.) long. Its area is one square unit.

Units: A word used with measurement. For example, metric units.

Unordered numbers: Numbers used for counting when the order does not matter, such as one, two, three, four, five and so on. Also called 'cardinal numbers' or 'counting numbers'. *See* Ordered numbers.

Vertical: Upright, perpendicular to the horizontal.

Volume: The size of a 3D shape. It is measured in cubic units (such as cm^3 or in^3) by counting how many unit cubes can be fitted into it. *See* Capacity.

Whole number: A number containing only complete units, not parts of units (it does not contain decimals or fractions).

Index